CREATIVE
leadlighting
a book of designs

PAUL DANAHER & DEXTER JACKSON

VIKING

Viking
Penguin Books Australia Ltd
487 Maroondah Highway, PO Box 257
Ringwood, Victoria 3134, Australia
Penguin Books Ltd
Harmondsworth, Middlesex, England
Penguin Putnam Inc.
375 Hudson Street, New York, New York 10014, USA
Penguin Books Canada Limited
10 Alcorn Avenue, Toronto, Ontario, Canada M4V 3B2
Penguin Books (NZ) Ltd
Cnr Rosedale and Airborne Roads, Albany, Auckland, New Zealand
Penguin Books (South Africa) (Pty) Ltd
5 Watkins Street, Denver Ext 4, 2094, South Africa
Penguin Books India (P) Ltd
11, Community Centre, Panchsheel Park, New Delhi, 110 017, India

First published by Penguin Books Australia Ltd 1999

10 9 8 7 6 5 4 3 2 1

Design by Melissa Fraser, Penguin Design Studio
Photography by Peter Suveges and Shane Hogarth
Printed and bound by South China Printing Co., Hong Kong, China

National Library of Australia
Cataloguing-in-Publication data:

Danaher, Paul.
    Creative leadlighting : a book of designs.

    ISBN 0 670 87547 3.

    1. Glass painting and staining – Australia. 2. Glass painting and staining –
    Australia – Patterns. I. Jackson, Dexter. II. Title.

748.50284

contents

preface

The essence of leadlighting is controlling light as it filters through glass of differing colours and textures, creating a unique fusion of light and art.

Much of the success of leadlighting as a hobby can be attributed to the fact that learning the craft itself is completely achievable. Indeed, broken down into its various stages, the construction of a leadlight panel loses much of its mystery. Cutting glass, assembling the pieces, soldering the lead joins and puttying and detailing a window – all of these tasks are usually mastered by hobbyists with the minimum of fuss, a little tuition, and a couple of bandaids. But creating a design is another matter …

Some people take to designing windows with ease and create new and refreshing designs of their own; however, many others would rather go to the dentist than create their own designs. Often they know exactly what they want, but putting it down on paper seems to be their stumbling block.

The Lead Balloon has been involved in manufacturing leadlights, conducting classes and retailing leadlight supplies since the late sixties. Over these years, Dexter and I have retained all of our working drawings, and it is these that form the basis of many of the designs presented here in *Creative Leadlighting*. You may rest assured, therefore, that these drawings are tried and true and are not full of shapes that are either impractical by nature or impossible to cut.

In this book, as well as in our previous books *Australian Leadlighting* and *Designs for Australian Leadlighting*, we have tried to make the task of designing your window easier by presenting a range of good-quality designs with which to inspire you. There are designs from the Victorian era featuring painted birds and borders. There are Edwardian designs, which include both Art Nouveau and Federation styles with their displays of flowers and softer, flowing lines. Art Deco designs with their clean, crisp geometry and heavily textured glass mixtures are also featured, as is a good selection of Australiana and contemporary designs.

It is intended that these designs be enlarged and reproduced in part or in full. You may care to mix and match elements of the various designs. Flowers, ribboning, backgrounds and borders can all be interchanged, and with a little time, patience and beer (or wine, if your prefer!), you should be able to design quality leadlight windows of your own.

If you are unsure if your design is practical, or you need help choosing materials or even some assistance with your cutting and leading, get friendly with the staff at your leadlight supplier. If you are buying your materials from them they should be more than happy to give you some of their time.

We hope that *Creative Leadlighting* stimulates your imagination and takes some of the pain out of choosing and designing your leadlight panel, regardless of whether you are a professional leadlighter or a hobbyist.

Good luck with your leadlighting.

CREATIVE
victorian

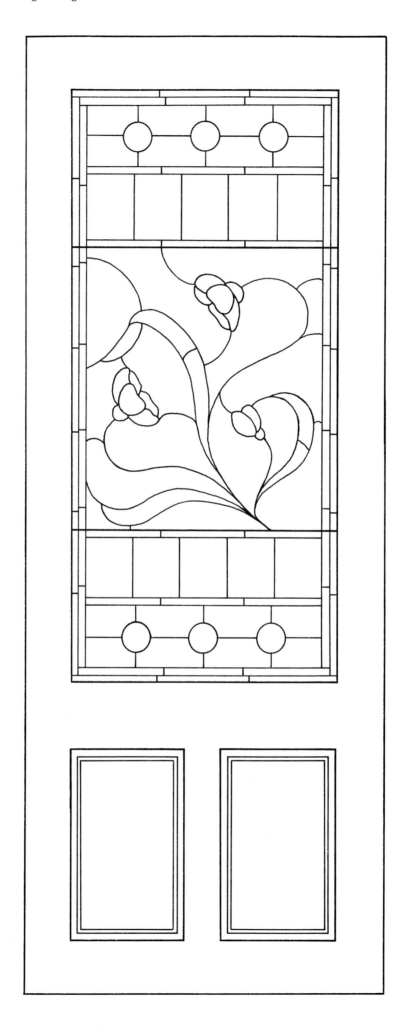

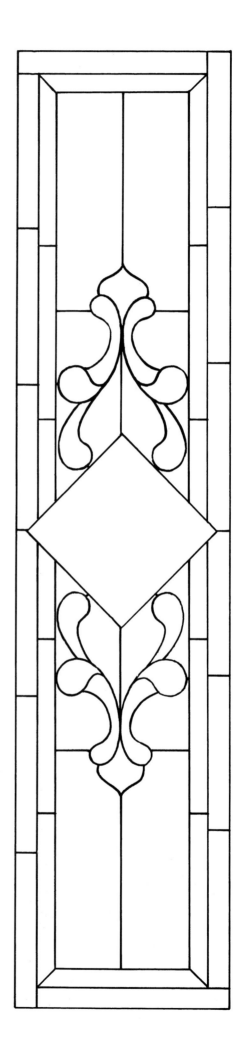

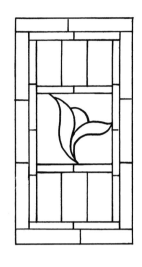

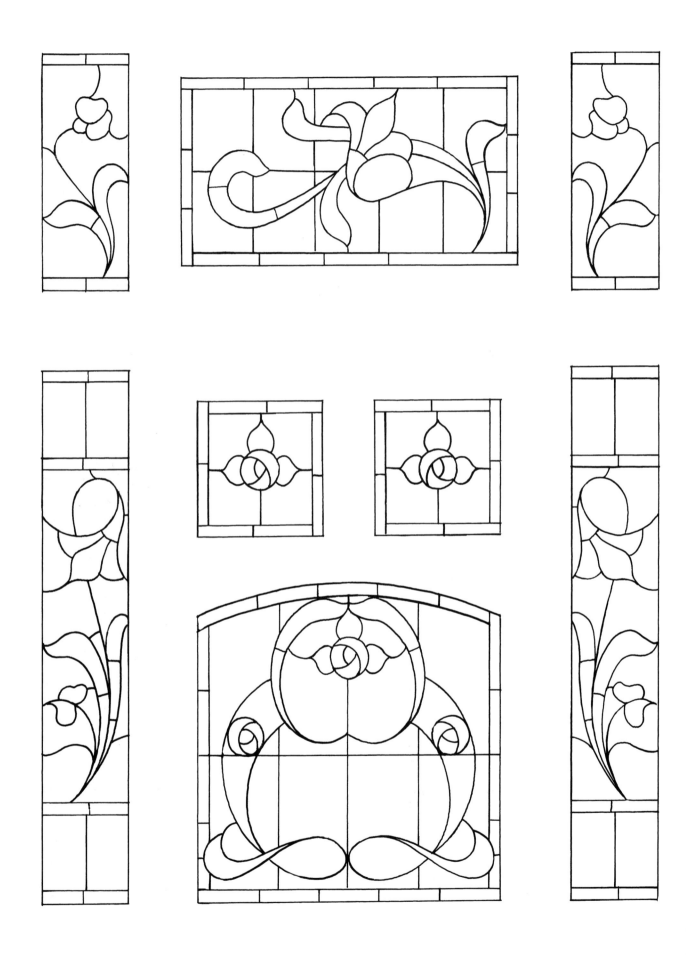

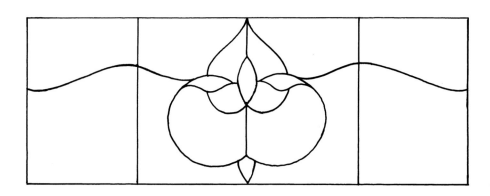

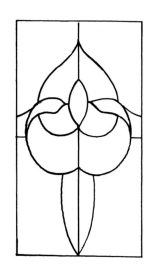

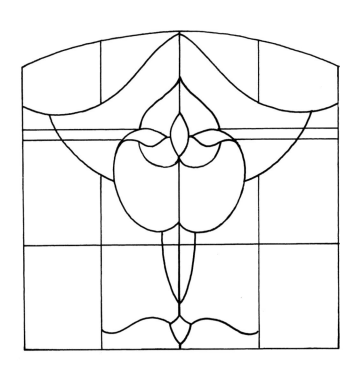

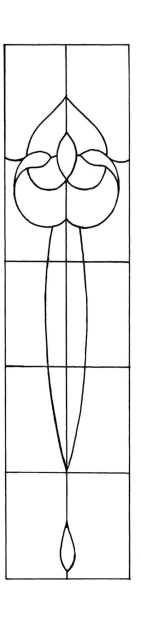

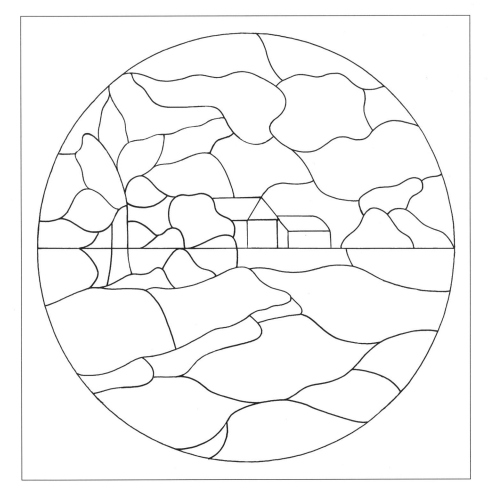

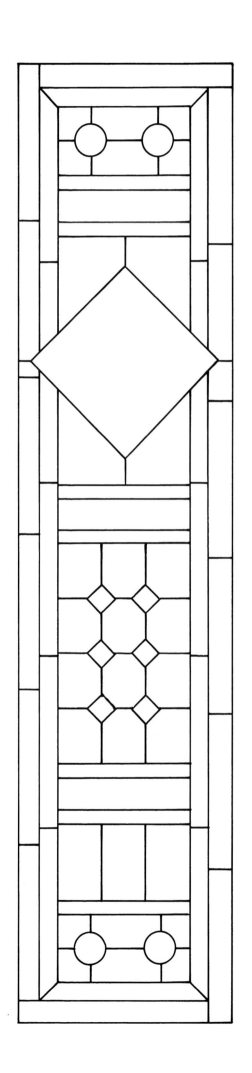

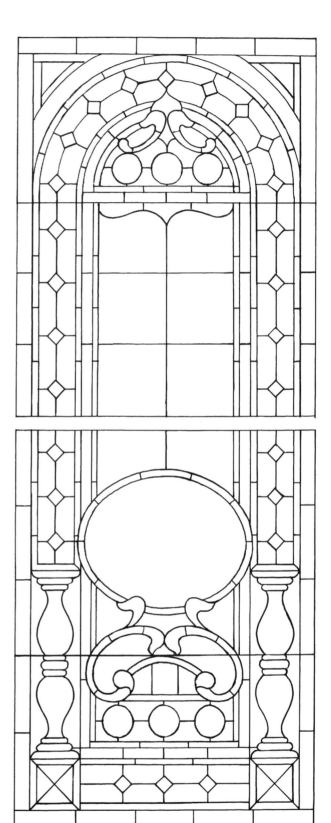

CREATIVE
edwardian

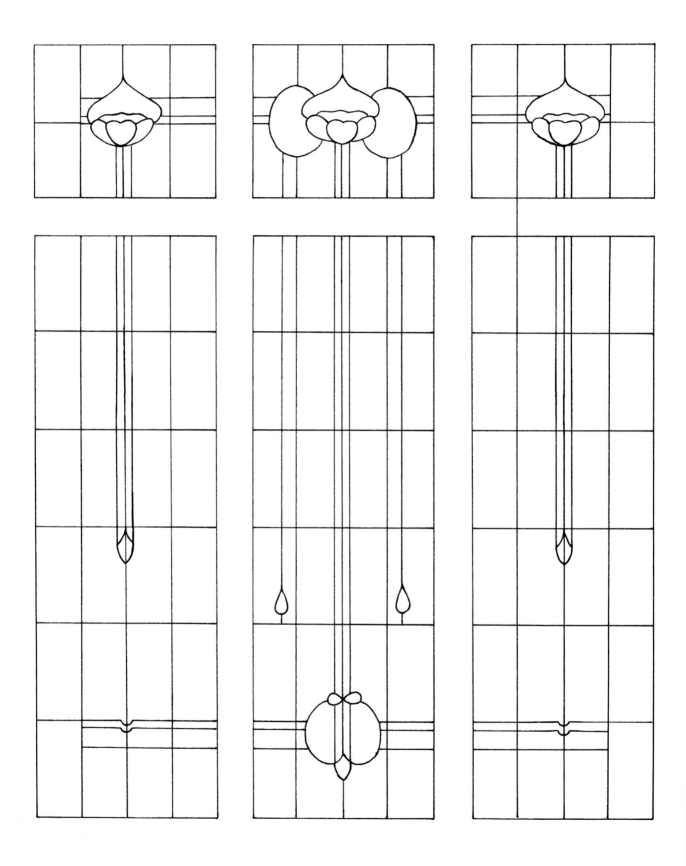

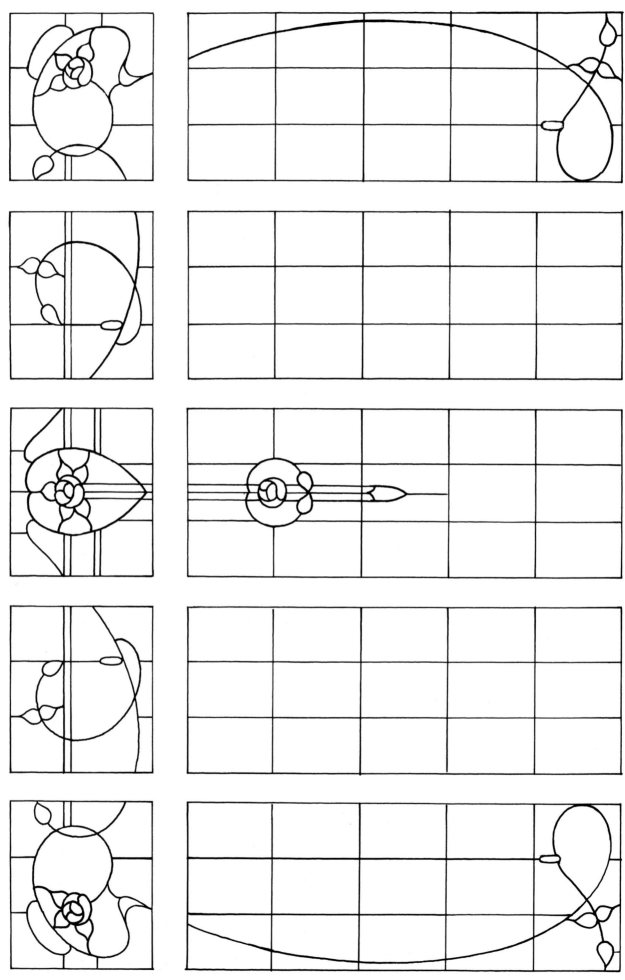

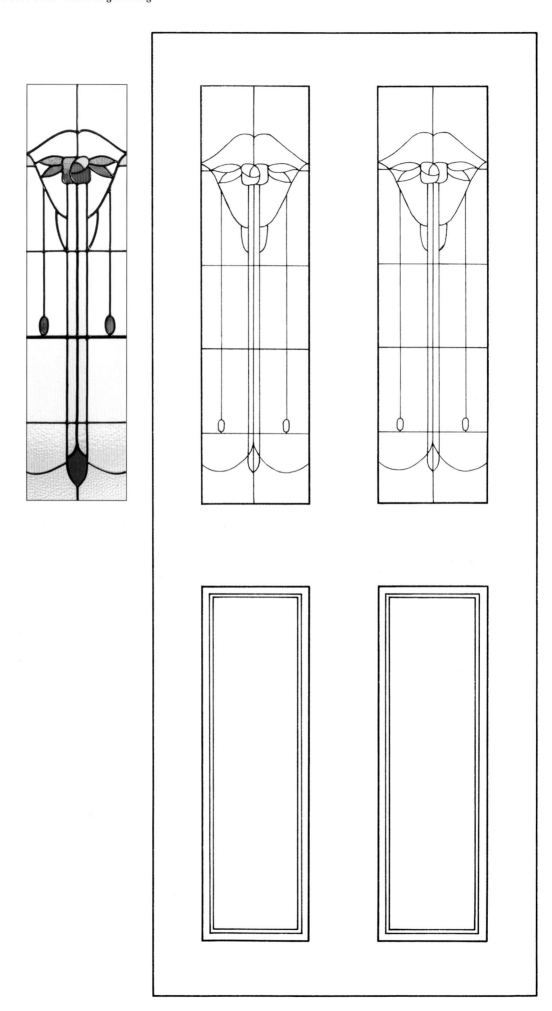

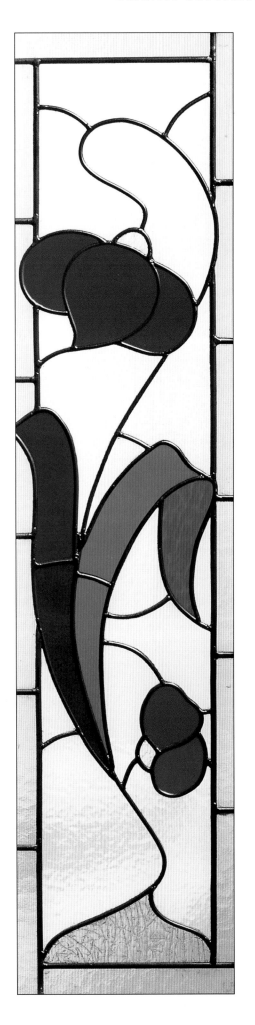

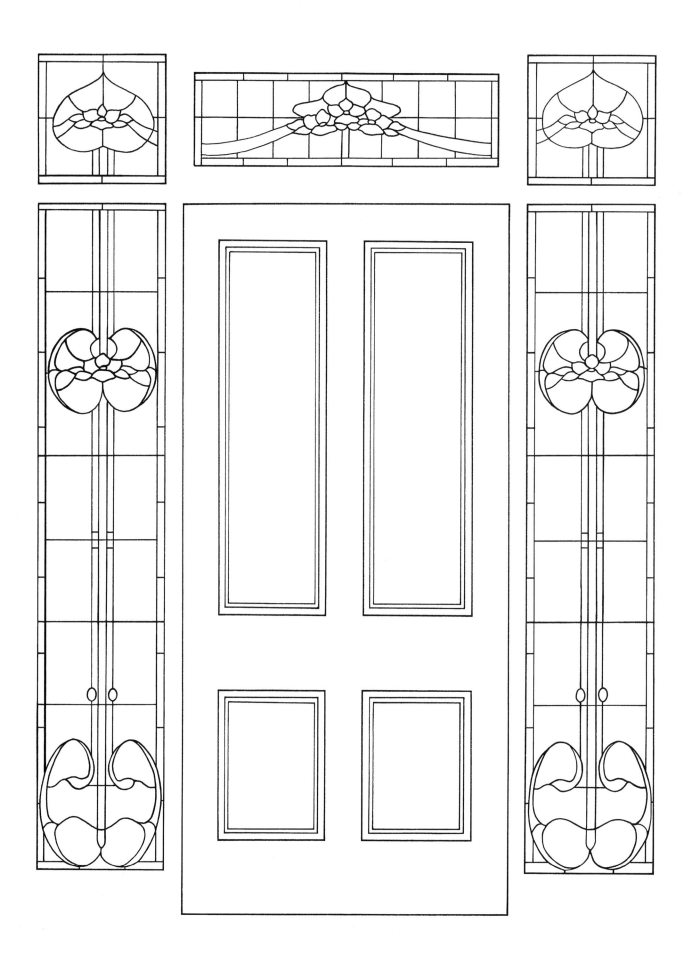

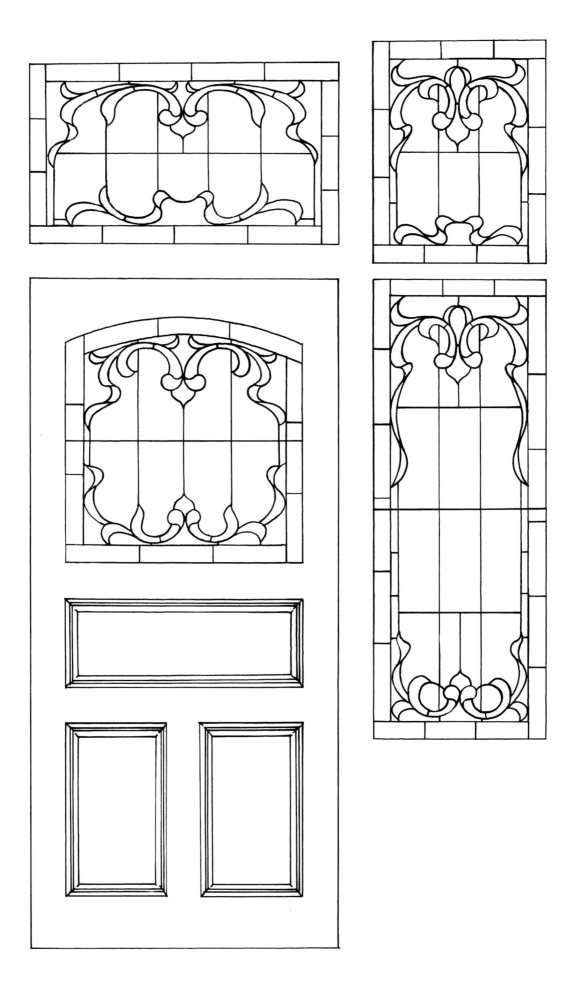

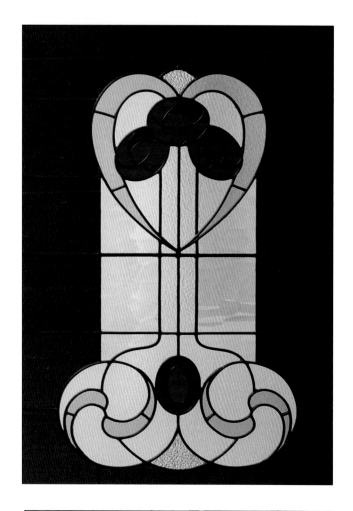

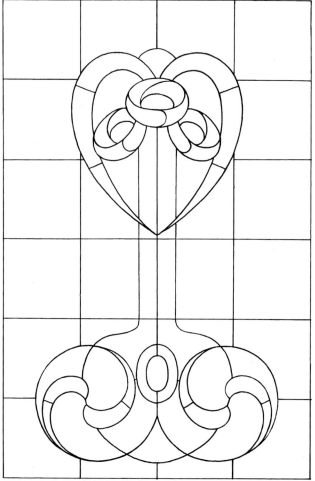

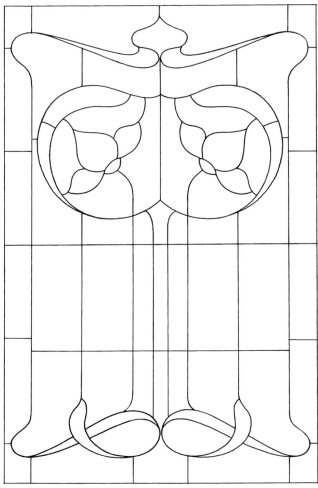

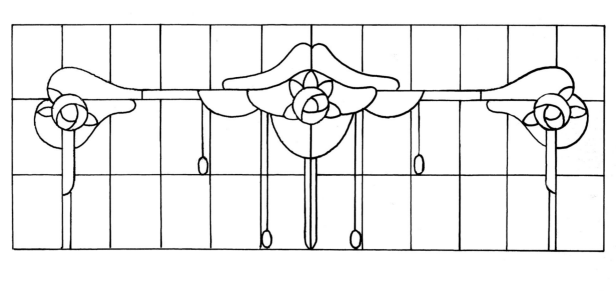

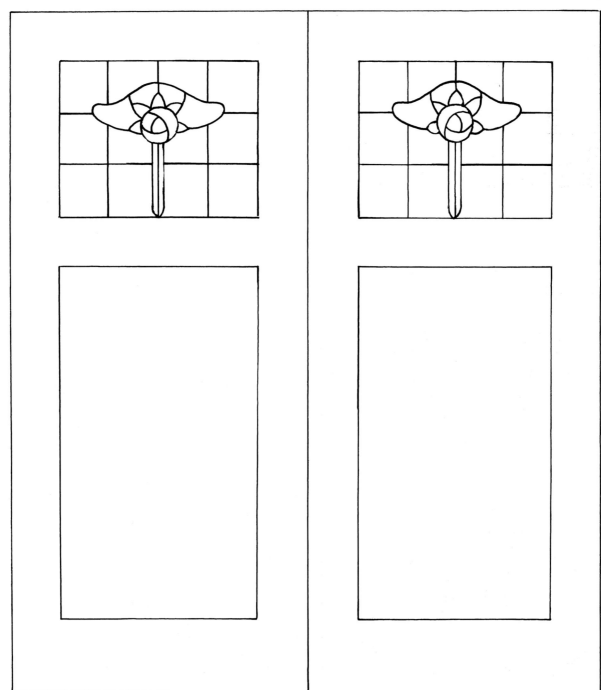

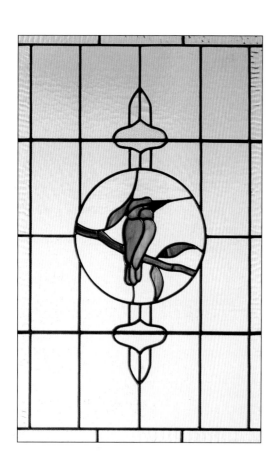

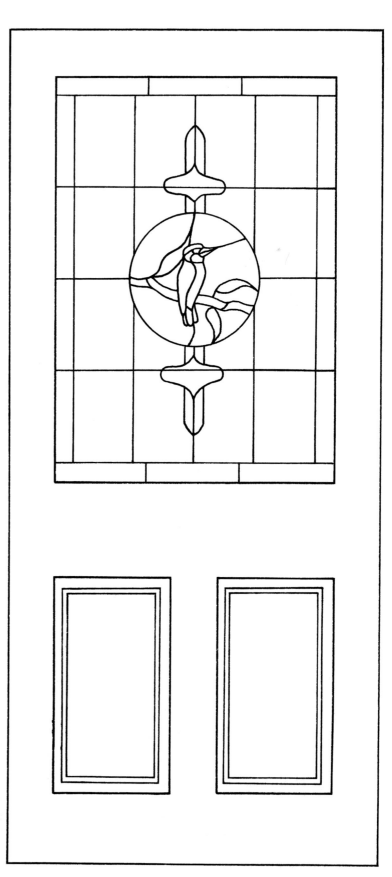

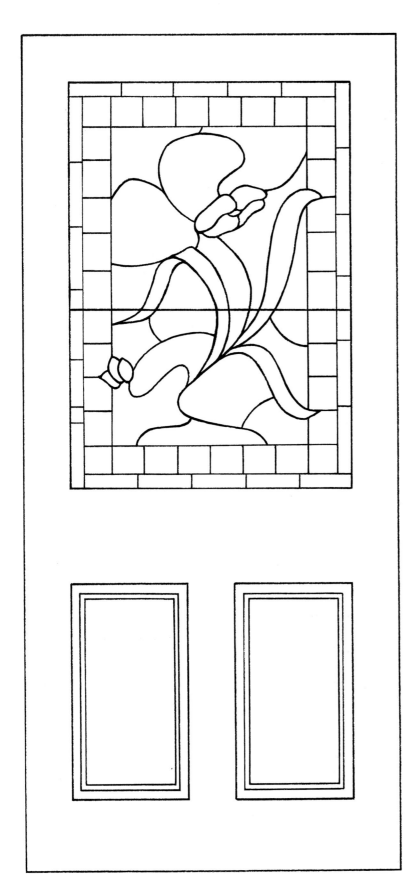

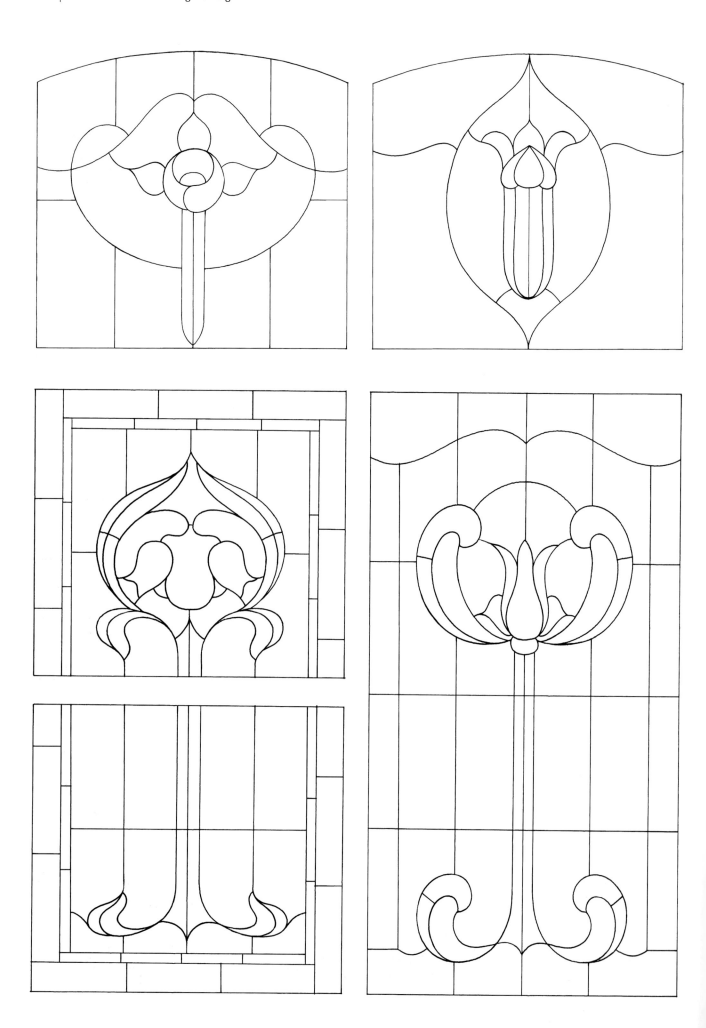

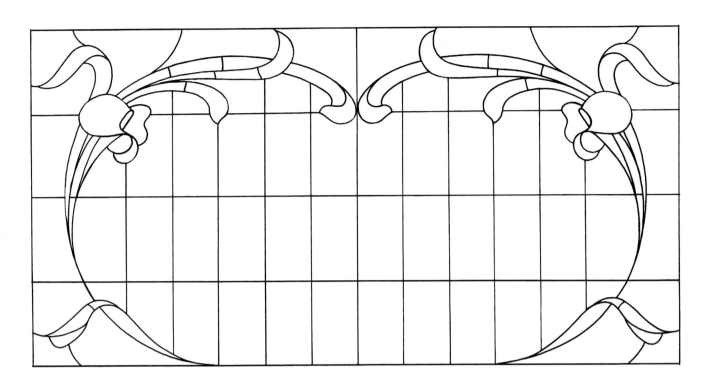

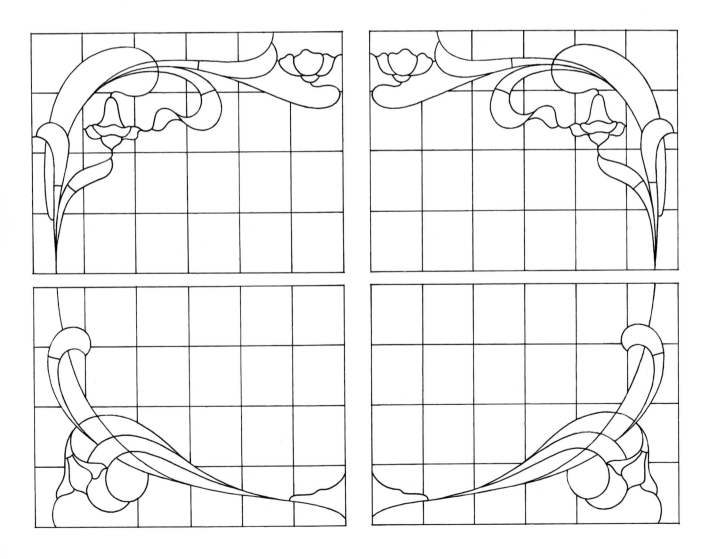

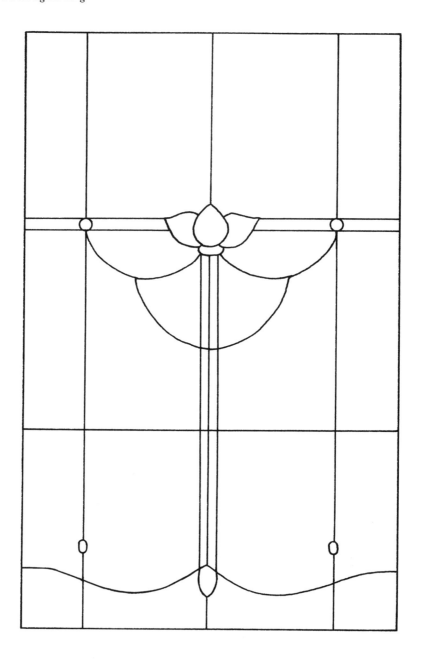

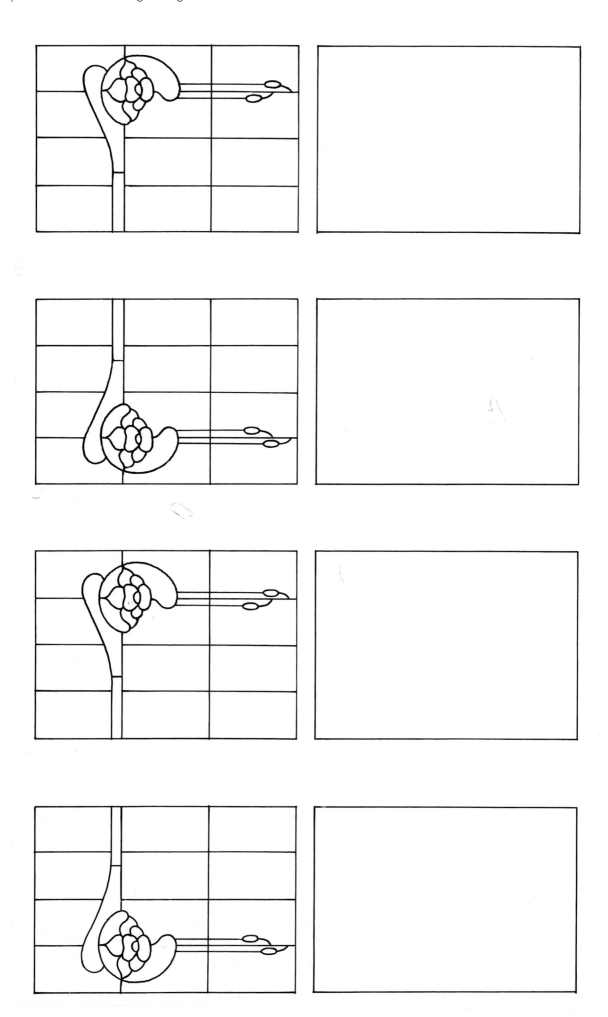

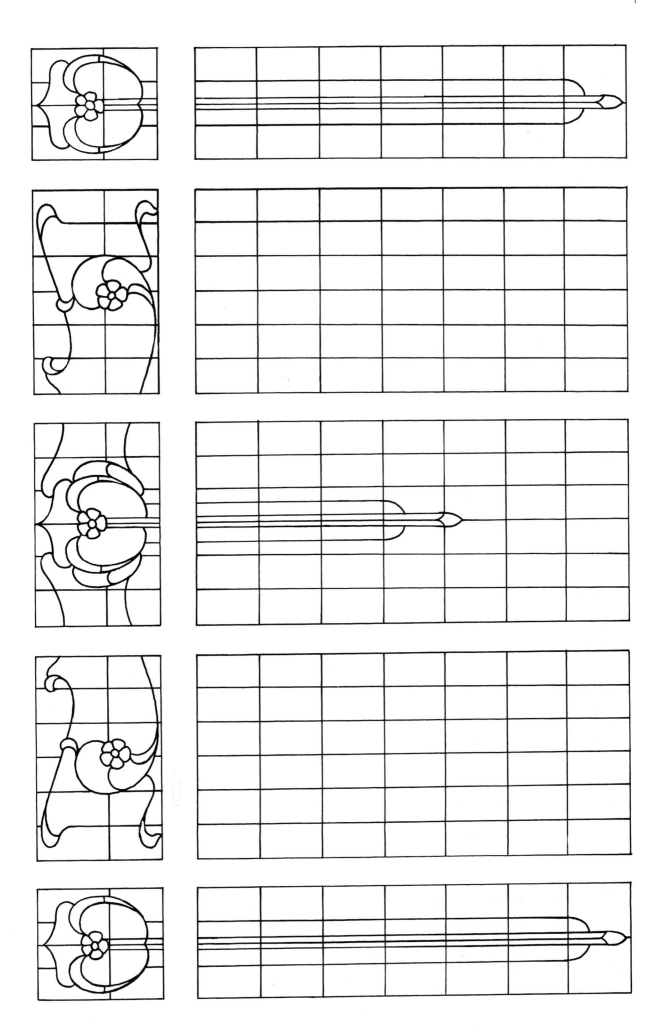

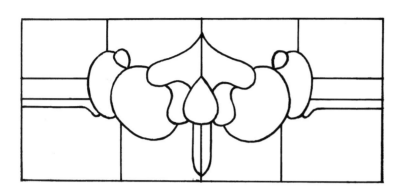

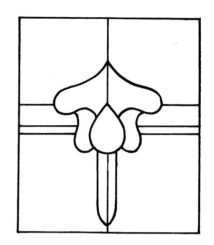

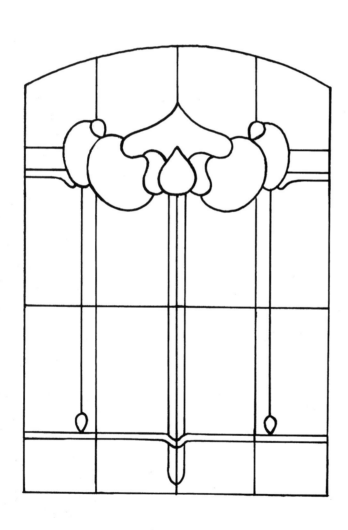

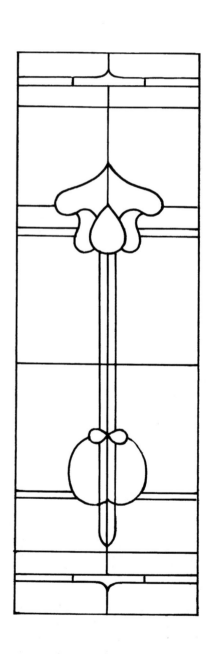

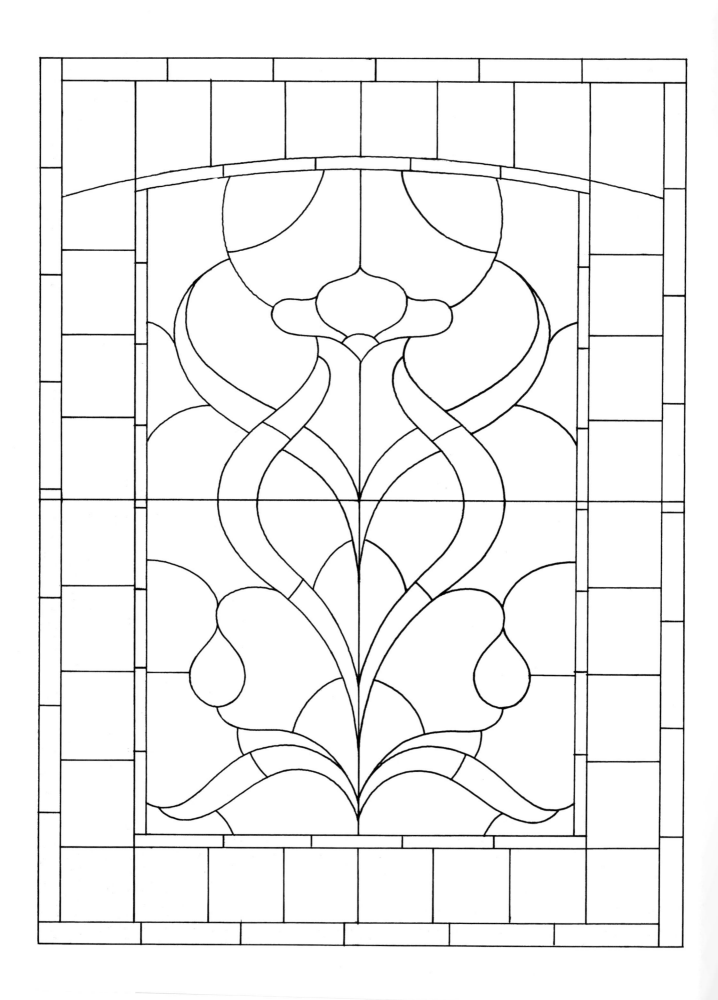

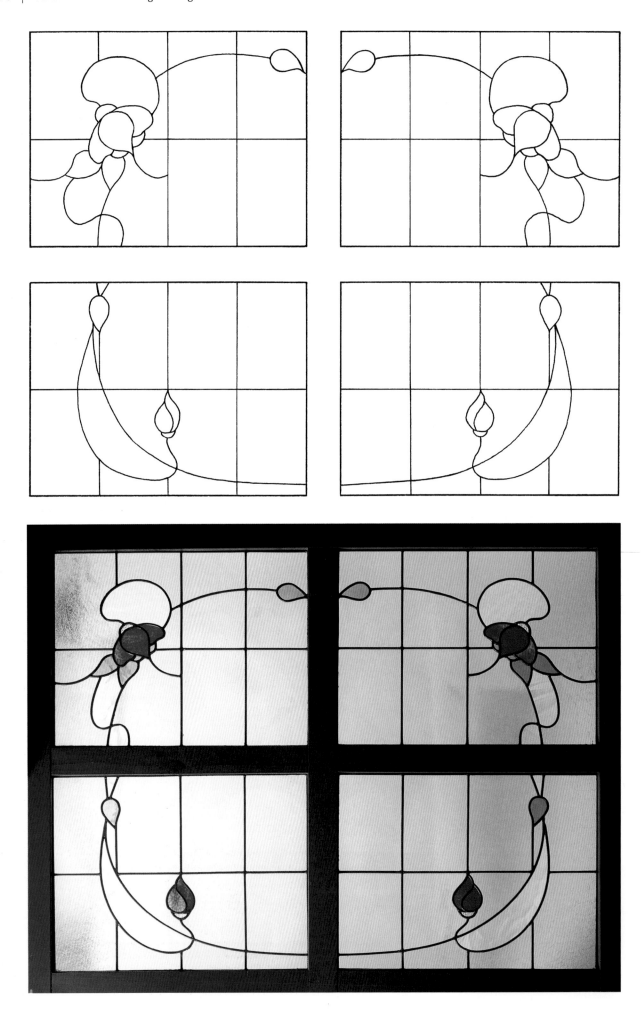

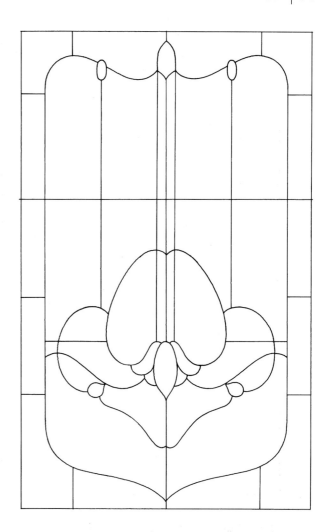

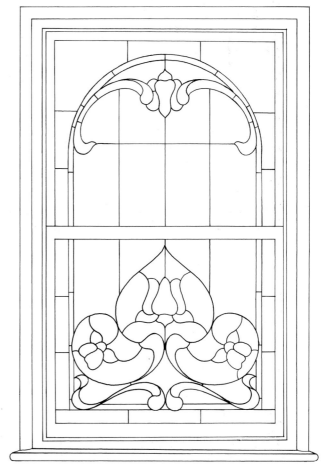

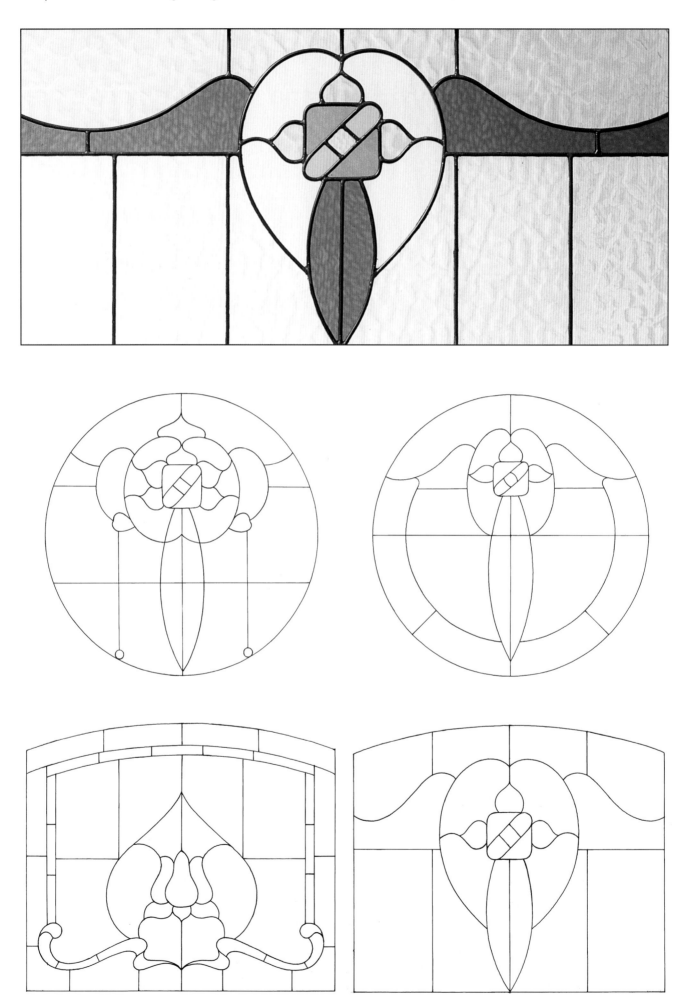

CREATIVE
art nouveau

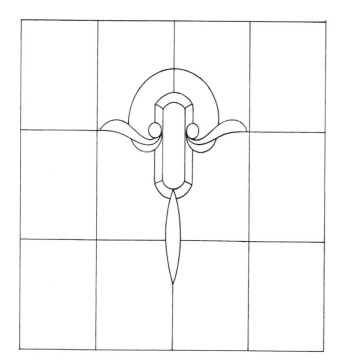

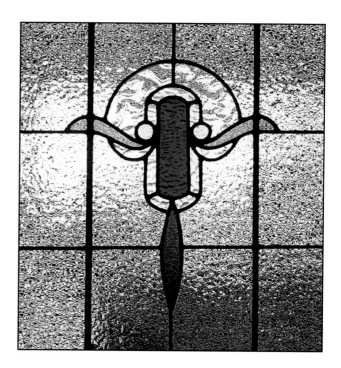

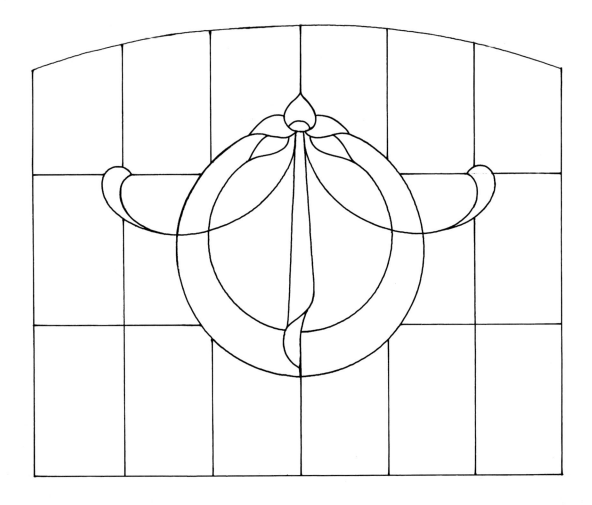

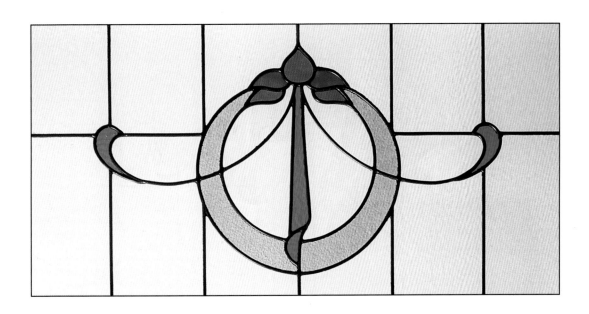

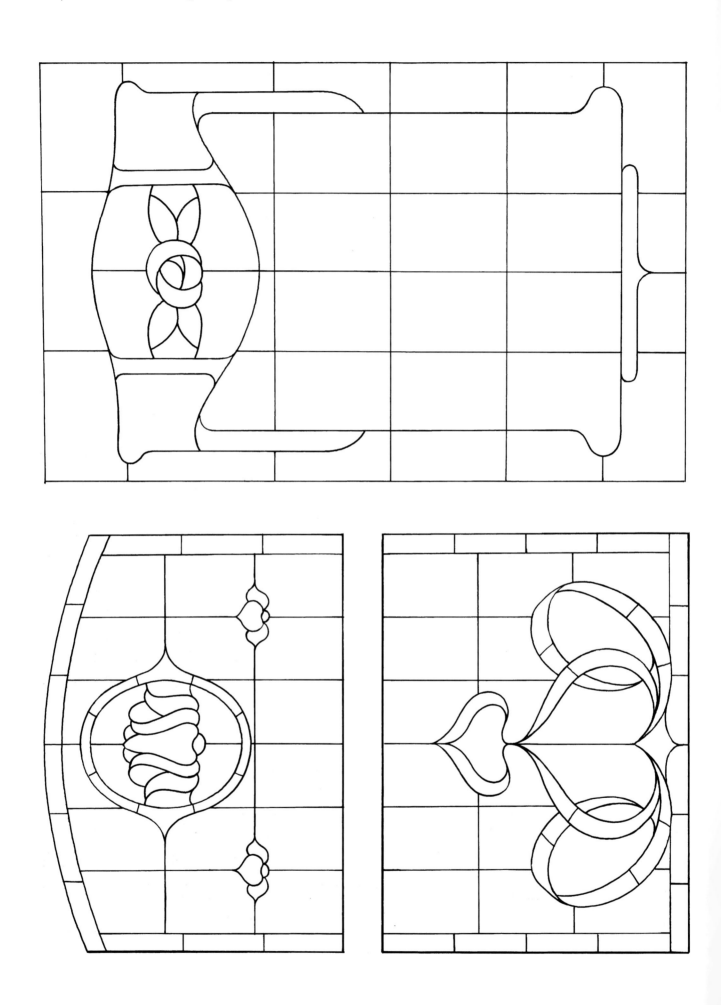

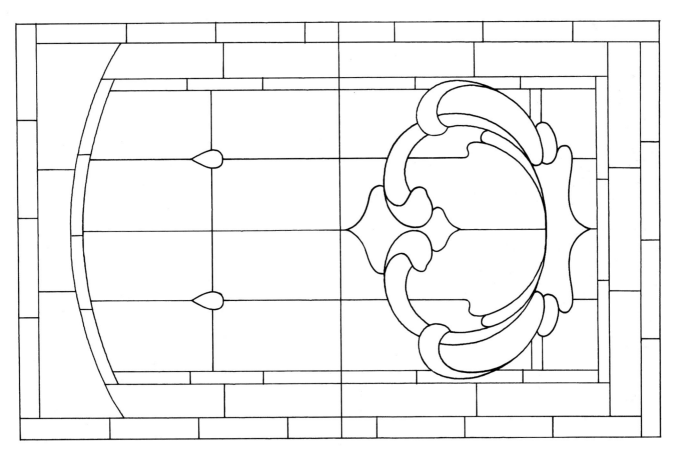

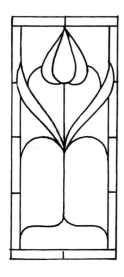

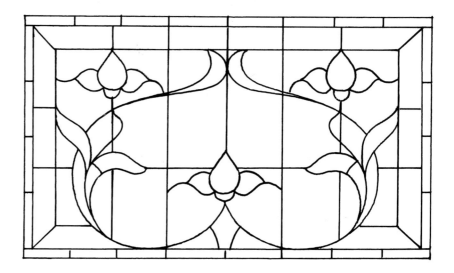

CREATIVE
art deco

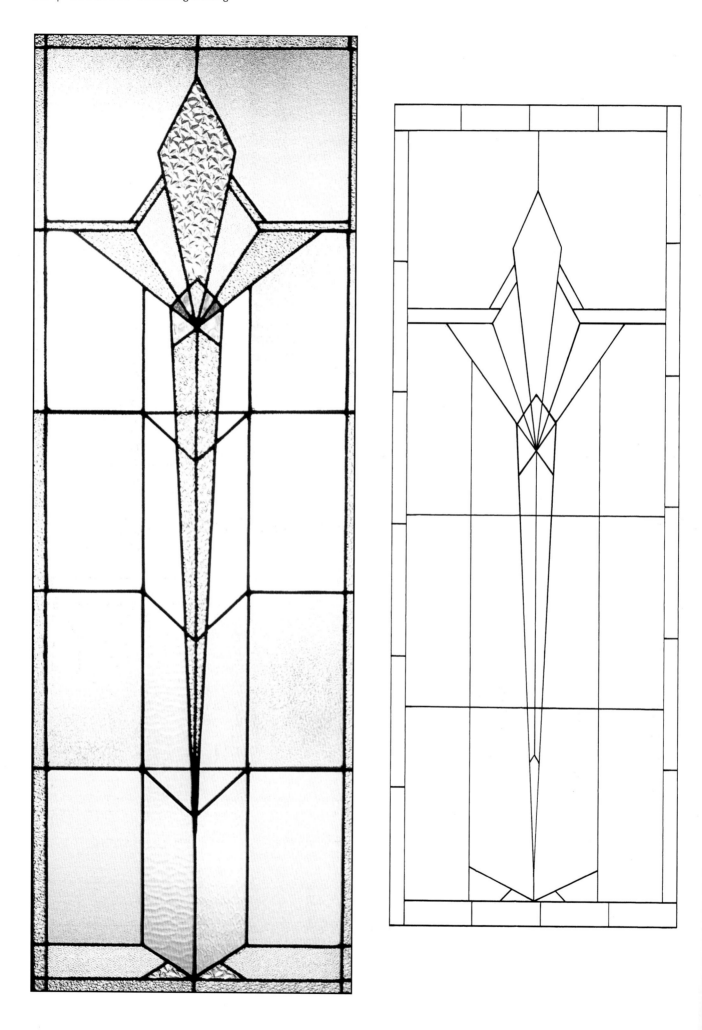

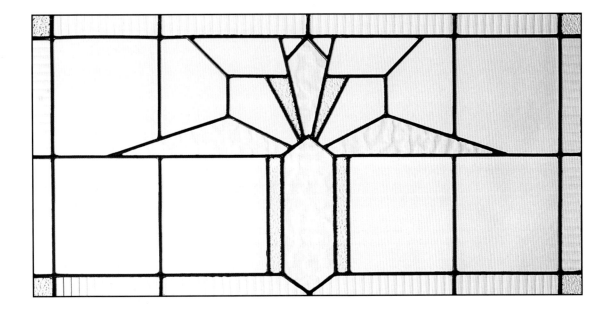

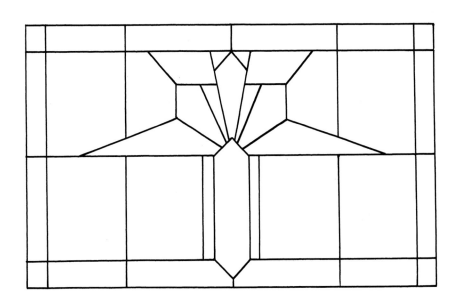
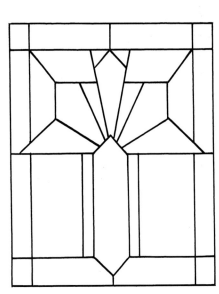

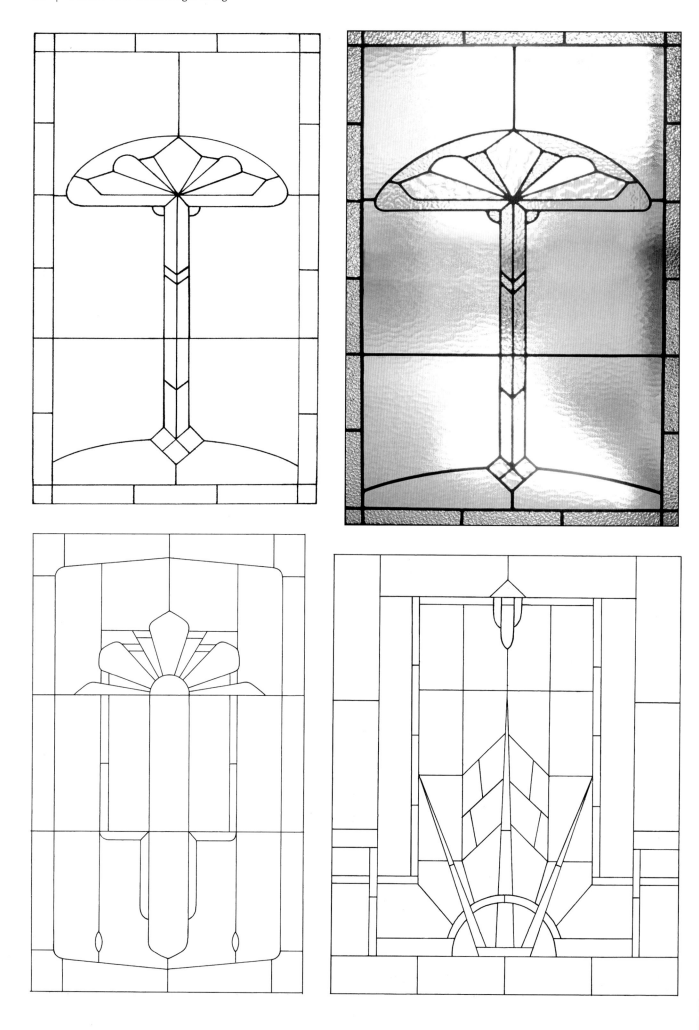

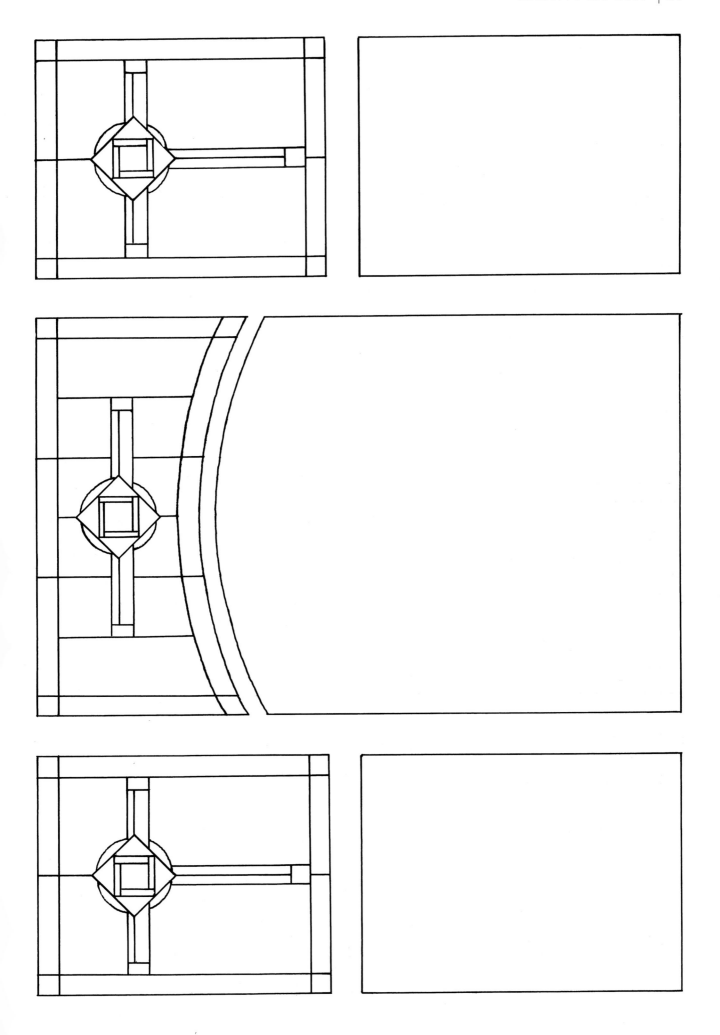

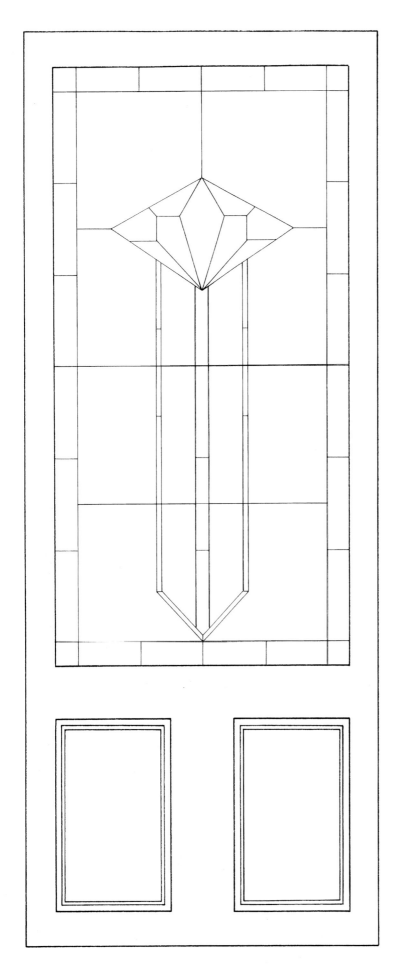

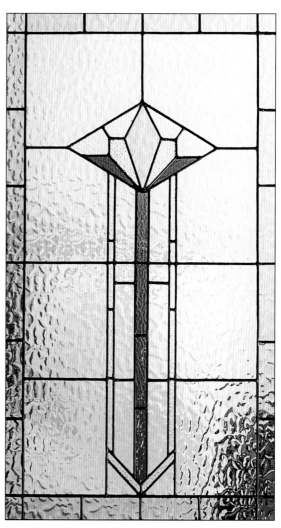

CREATIVE
contemporary

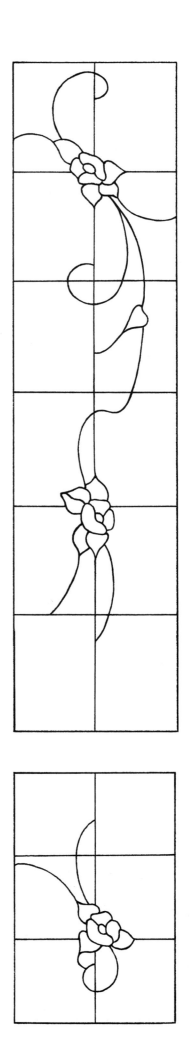

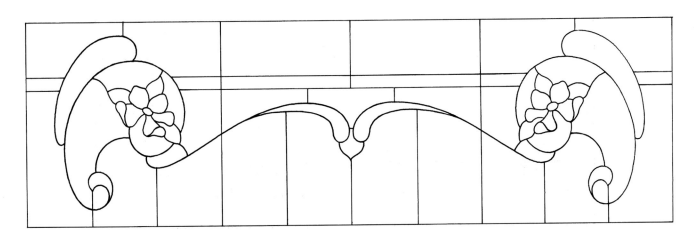

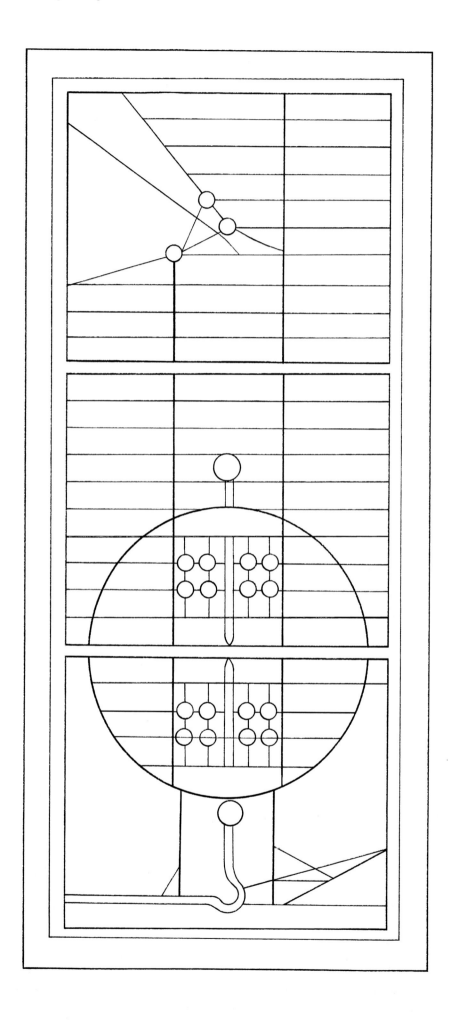

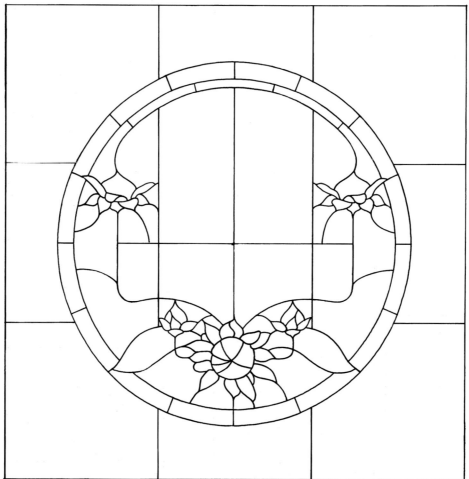

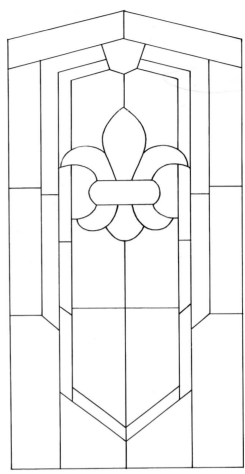
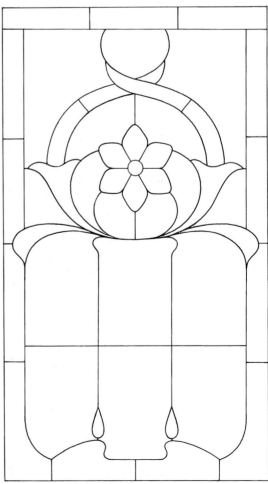

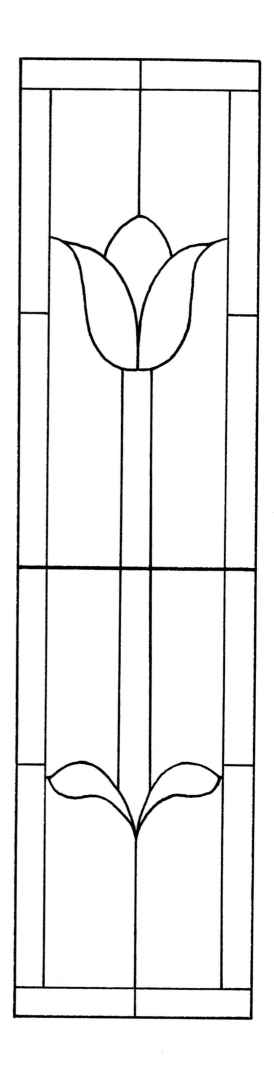

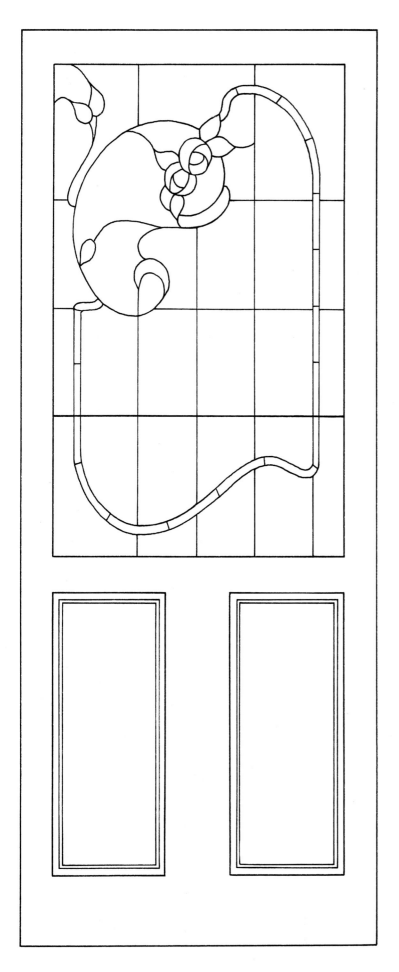

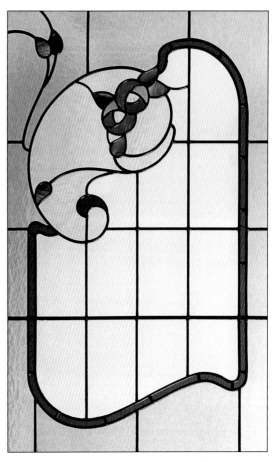

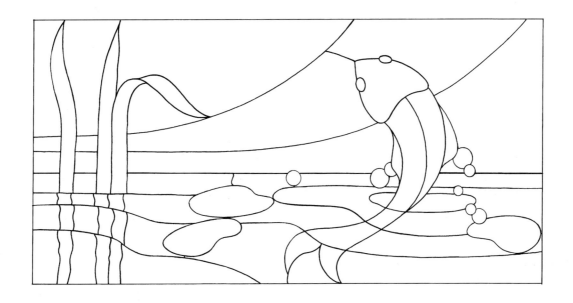

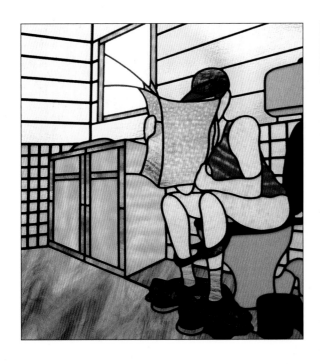

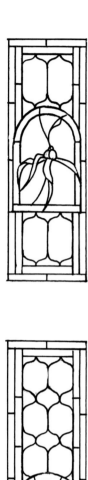
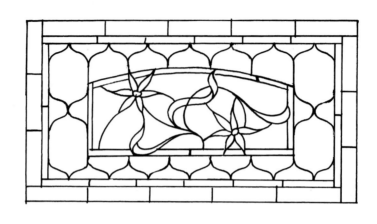

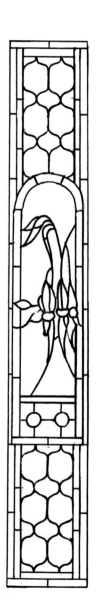